ARMORED
DINOSAURS!
The Ornithischians

WORLD
BOOK

A Scott Fetzer company
Chicago
www.worldbook.com

For information about other World Book publications, visit our website at http://www.worldbookonline.com or call **1-800-WORLDBK (967-5325)**.

For information about sales to schools and libraries, call **1-800-975-3250** (United States), or **1-800-837-5365** (Canada).

World Book, Inc.
233 N. Michigan Ave.
Chicago, IL 60601

Amber Books Ltd.
74-77 White Lion Street
London N1 9PF
United Kingdom
www.amberbooks.co.uk

Library of Congress Cataloging-in-Publication Data

Armored dinosaurs: the Ornithischians.
    p. cm. -- (Dinosaurs!)
    Summary: "An introduction to armored and duckbilled dinosaurs, plant-eating dinosaurs that belong to the group called ornithischians, one of the two major groups of dinosaurs. Features include an original drawing of each dinosaur, fun facts, a glossary, and a list of additional resources"--Provided by publisher.
    Includes index.
    ISBN 978-0-7166-0367-2
    1. Ornithischia--Juvenile literature. I. World Book, Inc.
    QE862.065A755 2013
    567.914--dc23
                    2012016106

Dinosaurs!
Set ISBN 978-0-7166-0366-5
Printed in China by Toppan Leefung Printing Ltd.,
Guangdong Province
1st printing September 2012

STAFF

Executive Committee

President
Donald D. Keller
Vice President and Editor in Chief
Paul A. Kobasa
Vice President of Sales & Marketing
Sean Lockwood
Vice President, International
Richard Flower
Director, Human Resources
Bev Ecker

Editorial

*Associate Director,
    Supplementary Publications*
Scott Thomas
*Managing Editor,
    Supplementary Publications*
Barbara A. Mayes
Editors
Michael Barr
Brian Johnson
Nicholas Kilzer
Kristina Vaicikonis
Researcher
Annie Brodsky
Administrative Assistant
Ethel Matthews
Manager, Indexing Services
David Pofelski
*Manager, Contracts & Compliance
    (Rights & Permissions)*
Loranne K. Shields

Editorial Administration

Director, Systems and Projects
Tony Tills
*Senior Manager,
    Publishing Operations*
Timothy Falk
*Associate Manager,
    Publishing Operations*
Audrey Casey

Manufacturing/Production

Director
Carma Fazio
Manufacturing Manager
Steven K. Hueppchen
Production/Technology Manager
Anne Fritzinger
Production Specialist
Curley Hunter
Proofreader
Emilie Schrage

Graphics and Design

Senior Manager
Tom Evans
Senior Designer
Don Di Sante

Product development
Amber Books Ltd.
Authors
Per Christiansen and Chris McNab
Designer
Jerry Williams

Contents

Introduction

It is a sunny day, about 67 million years ago, in what is now North Dakota. An Ankylosaurus calmly munches low-lying vegetation along the bank of a shallow river. Suddenly, a fierce Tyrannosaurus bursts through the trees. The Ankylosaurus immediately presses itself to the ground. The Tyrannosaurus lunges to bite, but it can do little damage to the thick, hard armor that protects the back of the Ankylosaurus. Then, the Ankylosaurus pivots and swings its clubbed tail, smashing it into the leg of Tyrannosaurus. The giant meat-eater turns tail and limps away, roaring in pain.

Such was life for the ornithischians (*AWR-nuh-THIHS-kee-uhns*), which are also known as the armored dinosaurs. They needed their armor, for these dinosaurs lived among the largest *predators* (meat-eaters) that ever roamed Earth. There were four main types of ornithischians: (1) ankylosaurs (2) stegosaurs, (3) ceratopsians, (4) and hadrosaurs.

Each of these groups thrived for millions of years. Ankylosaurs (*ANG-kuh-luh-sawrz*) had broad heads, tanklike armored bodies, and heavy, clubbed tails. Stegosaurs (*STEHG-uh-sawrz*) grew two rows of spikes or plates along their back and tail. The ceratopsians (*SEHR-uh-TOP-see-uhns*) were horned dinosaurs, resembling rhinoceroses. They had a parrotlike beak and a large bony frill extending across the neck from the back of the skull. The hadrosaurs (*HAD-ruh-sawrz*), often called duckbilled dinosaurs, had a broad, ducklike beak at the front of the mouth. Some sported impressive

Preserved skin impressions of a hadrosaur *(above)* show that these dinosaurs had thick skin with a pebbly texture. The fossil skeleton of a large hadrosaur called Parasaurolophus *(opposite)* displays an impressive head crest. The head crest was probably used to make loud honking calls.

head crests. Unlike other ornithischians, hadrosaurs lacked armor. Instead, they lived in herds for protection.

Armored giants lived throughout the Age of Dinosaurs—251 million to 65 million years ago. During this period, Earth went through great changes. In the beginning, a vast supercontinent that scientists call Pangaea *(pan-JEE-uh)* was surrounded by a great ocean. Pangaea broke apart over millions of years, and the continents began to drift toward the positions they occupy today. Early in the Age of Dinosaurs, such seed plants as conifers, cycads, and ginkgoes were common; flying reptiles—pterosaurs *(TEHR-uh-sawrz)*—filled the skies; the oceans teemed with Plesiosaurs *(PLEE-see-uh-sawrz)* and other marine reptiles; birds arose from small meat-eating dinosaurs; and the first snakes appeared, along with modern bony fish.

The Age of Dinosaurs

Period	Triassic	Jurassic	Cretaceous
Began	251 million years ago	200 million years ago	145 million years ago
Ended	200 million years ago	145 million years ago	65 million years ago
Major Events	Dinosaurs first appeared but did not become common until the end of this period.	Dinosaurs became the largest animals everywhere on land, reaching their greatest size.	A mass extinction at the end of this period killed off all the dinosaurs except some birds.

Dinosaurs first appeared during the Triassic Period. They became the largest, most successful land animals early in the Jurassic Period. The dinosaurs died out at the end of the Cretaceous Period. Together, these three periods make up the Mesozoic Era, the Age of Dinosaurs.

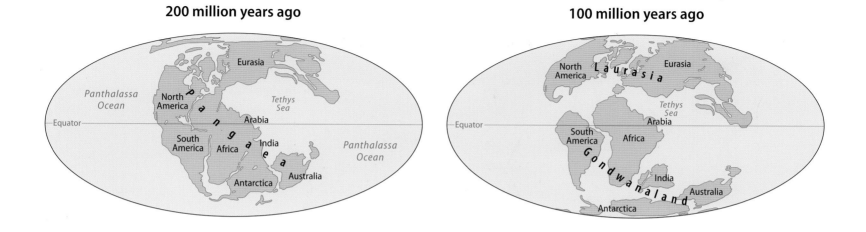

200 million years ago

100 million years ago

About 200 million years ago *(above left)* a supercontinent that scientists call Pangaea was surrounded by a vast ocean. Pangaea broke up into separate continents during the Age of Dinosaurs. By 100 million years ago *(above right),* the continents had begun to drift toward the positions they occupy today.

Some ornithisichians thrived during these changes, while others struggled to adapt. The stegosaurs had all but disappeared by the Cretaceous Period. Scientists are not sure why they went into decline, but they may have struggled to compete with other plant-eating dinosaurs. The ankylosaurs, ceratopsians, and hadrosaurs are among the most common fossils of dinosaurs from the Cretaceous Period. They flourished right up until the end of the Age of Dinosaurs, about 65 million years ago. At this time, the dinosaurs became extinct. The armored giants that once roamed the land have all died, but we can reconstruct their world through the fossils they left behind.

Ankylosaurs

Many ankylosaurs had a bony club at the end of the tail for defense *(right)*. Others lacked this weapon but were protected by their sharp spikes *(opposite)*.

The ankylosaurs were the most heavily armored of all dinosaurs. They needed a lot of protection because they lived in a world full of fierce meat-eating dinosaurs. Ankylosaurs were low, broad animals that walked on four legs. This made it almost impossible for predators to tip them over and attack their soft bellies. Most ankylosaurs had heavy, bony plates embedded in the skin across their back, tail, and head. Many of the plates had ridges or spikes. In some ankylosaurs, large spikes also grew at the shoulders or at the back of the head. Some even had armored eyelids! Many ankylosaurs had a large mass of bone at the end of the tail. This bone could be used as a powerful club to defend against predators.

Although most ankylosaurs were large and walked on all fours, some early kinds were much smaller and lightly armored. These early ankylosaurs could probably move about on either two or four legs.

Ankylosaurs lived in many parts of the world from the early Jurassic Period to the end of the Cretaceous Period. These tanklike animals were some of the most successful plant-eating dinosaurs. They ate the leaves of ferns and low-growing plants that they sheared off with their pointed, horny beaks. The ankylosaurs died out with other dinosaurs at the end of the Cretaceous Period, about 65 million years ago.

Dracopelta

(drack-oh-PELL-ta)

Dracopelta could rely on its bony covering and sharp body spikes for protection from attack. This small, early ankylosaur may have rolled into an armored ball when attacked.

Hylaeosaurus

(hi-LEE-oh-SAWR-us)

Hylaeosaurus was the first ankylosaur fossil found in the United Kingdom, in 1832. It weighed up to about 1 ton (0.9 metric ton) and was heavily armored, with bony plates and spikes.

Emausaurus

(EE-mau-SAWR-us)

Emausaurus had leaf-shaped teeth that it used to pull large amounts of leaves from branches. Much of its body was covered in bony scales.

Scelidosaurus (SKEL-eye-doh-SAWR-us)

was a small, armored dinosaur that lived about 200 million years ago. Scientists have found its fossils in Asia, Europe, and North America. It was among the earliest ankylosaurs.

FACT O SAUR

Sir Richard Owen was a British scientist who named Scelidosaurus in 1860. He also coined the term "dinosaur"—"terrible lizard"—in 1842.

Scelidosaurus shared its environment with a number of large predators, but its armor plates would have made it difficult to attack.

Scelidosaurus bit off ferns and shrubs with its strong beak. It probably did not chew its food much because its jaws could only move up and down rather than sideways.

Scelidosaurus probably moved slowly on its four sturdy legs. Each foot ended in four toes with hooflike claws.

11

Polacanthus

(pole-ah-CAN-thus)
Polacanthus weighed about
1 ton (0.9 metric ton). It had
evenly spaced rows of spikes
along its sides and on its
shoulders.

Minmi

(MIN-mee)
Fossils of Minmi were first
discovered in Queensland,
Australia. This small, early
ankylosaur is known from
several nearly complete
skeletons.

Nodosaurus

(NODE-oh-SAWR-us)
Nodosaurus means "knobbly
lizard." These armored giants were
given their name because of their
hard shell of knob-covered bony
plates. Nodosaurus and its close
relatives lacked a bony club at the
end of the tail.

Saichania

(siy-KAHN-ee-ah)
Saichania had empty chambers in its skull, which suggests that it had an excellent sense of smell. These spaces also may have allowed it to roar loudly.

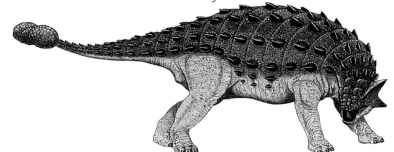

Struthiosaurus

STROO-thee-oh-SAWR-us
Struthiosaurus is the smallest armored dinosaur known. An adult measured about 6 feet (2 meters) long from head to tail.

Talarurus

(TAL-a-RU-rus)
Large meat-eaters probably thought twice before attacking Talarurus. Biting through Talarurus's bony plates would have been difficult. This dinosaur could also swing the club on its tail like a hammer to smash even the thick bones of a big attacker.

FUN FACT

The tail of Talarurus had tissues interwoven like a basket. This provided great power and strength when swinging the tail against an attacker.

Euoplocephalus

(*YOU-oh-plo-SEF-ah-lus*)
Euoplocephalus had a crushing disc-shaped tail club that weighed more than 30 pounds (13.6 kilograms).

Panoplosaurus

PAN-oh-ploh-SAWR-us
Like most ankylosaurs, Panoplosaurus had a toothless beak for feeding on low plants. It was a massive animal, weighing up to 3 ½ tons (3.2 metric tons).

FUN FACT

The skull of Panoplosaurus shows it likely had fleshy cheek pouches. These were used to hold plant matter, which the animal chewed slowly but constantly.

Edmontonia

(*ed-mon-TOE-nee-ah*)
Edmontonia had two huge spines on each shoulder. One pointed forward to protect the head and neck. The other pointed backward to protect the sides. With no club on the tail, this armored ankylosaur may have faced predators head-on.

Ankylosaurus had a globe-shaped club on the tail that was nearly the same size as its head. It could swing this club with great force.

Ankylosaurus lived in North America, from 68 million to 65 million years ago. Its massive armor helped to protect it from such huge meat-eating dinosaurs as Tyrannosaurus.

Ankylosaurus (ANG-kuh-luh-SAWR-us)

was built like a tank! Its head and back were covered with bony plates and long spikes, and it had a intimidating bone club at the end of its tail.

Ankylosaurus was the largest armored dinosaur. It grew to about 33 feet (10 meters) long and weighed up to 8 tons (7.3 metric tons).

FACT○SAUR

When attacked, Ankylosaurus may have pressed itself to the ground. In this position, the attacker could only bite or claw at the tough armor.

Learn more at www.worldbook.com/dino11

Stegosaurs

Stegosaurs kept their long, horselike skull *(below)* low to the ground, to feed on low-growing plants. These dinosaurs had a large, heavy body and walked on all fours. The hindlimbs were longer than the forelimbs, which gave them a highly arched back *(opposite)*.

The stegosaurs were a striking group of dinosaurs. Some of them looked odd, with a heavy body, a small head, long hind legs, and large plates sticking up from the back. Indeed, the name stegosaur means "roof reptile," because the large plates resemble roof tiles. However, not all stegosaurs had plates on their back. Some had long spikes running along their back and tail.

Some scientists believe that the plates and spikes of stegosaurs were used for defense against predators. Others suggest that the plates helped to control the animals' body temperature. According to this idea, blood passed through the thin plates, where it was cooled by air moving around the stegosaur's back. In this way, the dinosaur could lower its body temperature. The plates could also have helped to warm the blood by absorbing heat from the sun.

Stegosaurs had weak teeth in their long, narrow head. Their short front legs kept the head near the ground, and scientists think stegosaurs fed mainly on soft, low-growing ferns. These dinosaurs reached their peak in the Jurassic Period, but only a few kinds survived into the Cretaceous Period. Scientists are not sure why stegosaurs died out. However, they suspect that stegosaurs may have struggled to compete with other plant-eating dinosaurs.

Lexovisaurus

(lek-SOH-vee-SAWR-us)
Lexovisaurus was an early, medium-sized stegosaur that lived about 164 million years ago in what are now England and France.

Huayangosaurus

(hwah-YANG-oh-SAWR-us)
Huayangosaurus was an early stegosaur known from Jurassic fossils found in China. It has many primitive features and may be an ancestor to stegosaurs that appeared later.

Chialingosaurus

(CHEE-ah-LING-ah-SAWR-us)
Chialingosaurus was a medium-sized early stegosaur known from China. It probably ate soft, low-growing ferns and plants called cycads, which were plentiful in the Jurassic Period.

FACT○SAUR

Although Stegosaurus was huge, it had a tiny brain. Its brain was only about the size of a golf ball.

Stegosaurus (STEHG *uh* SAWR *uhs*)

was the largest of the stegosaurs, growing to 30 feet (9 meters) in length and weighing about 3 tons (2.7 metric tons). It lived in what are now Europe and North America.

Two rows of large, triangle-shaped plates lined the back of Stegosaurus. Some plates were more than 3 feet (1 meter) long.

Stegosaurus had a tiny, narrow head. Its toothless beak cropped plants low to the ground. It also had small, leaf-shaped teeth at the back of its mouth.

The end of the tail had four long, pointed spikes. Stegosaurus could swing these spikes at predators that dared to attack it.

Learn more at www.worldbook.com/dino12

Kentrosaurus

(KEN-troh-SAWR-us)
Kentrosaurus is known from fossils in Africa. It had plates and spikes along its back and tail, and two more spikes jutting out from its hips. The hip spikes protected the dinosaur's sides from attack.

Dacentrurus

(dah-sen-TROO-rus)
Dacentrurus had two rows of plates along its back and long spikes on its tail. The razor-sharp tail spikes were effective defensive weapons against predators.

Wuerhosaurus (*woo-AYR-hoh-SAWR-us*) was among the last of the plated dinosaurs. It is known from fossils found in China that date to the early Cretaceous Period. Nearly all other stegosaurs had already become extinct earlier, by the end of the Jurassic Period.

FACT O SAUR

Wuerhosaurus may have had its armored plates arranged in matching pairs. Other stegosaurs had plates in alternating pairs.

The plates on the back were longer and more rectangular than those that grew on Stegosaurus.

Wuerhosaurus had a small head, wide hips, short forelegs, and a highly arched back.

21

Ceratopsians

The horned ceratopsians *(SEHR-uh-TOP-see-uhns)* are some of the most famous dinosaurs. Most people recognize Triceratops *(try SEHR uh tops)* as soon as they see it. However, not all ceratopsian dinosaurs were so large and distinctive. Such early ceratopsians as Psittacosaurus *(SIT-ah-co-SAWR-us)* were tiny and walked on long hindlimbs. But even they had the parrotlike beak and wide head seen in later ceratopsians.

Scientists think horned dinosaurs originated in what is now Asia, where the oldest of these fossils have been found. These animals, known as protoceratopsians, then spread to what is now North America, where they thrived. There, they developed into a variety of animals about the size of rhinos or elephants. They had strong bodies, with short and muscular legs. Their large heads had horns on the nose and above the eyes, with a bony frill protecting the neck.

Triceratops is the most famous ceratopsian, and it was among the most successful. Its long horns, bony frill, and large size helped to protect it from such meat-eating dinosaurs as Tyrannosaurus. Triceratops likely roamed in great herds across western North America, about 65 million years ago.

A ceratopsian's massive head *(above)* had a bony frill that covered the neck. The frill provided protection for the dinosaur's vulnerable neck, as it chomped on plants with its parrotlike beak *(opposite)*.

Brachyceratops

(BRACK-ee-SAIR-uh-tops)

Fossils of this ceratopsian are found in North America. Only fossils of the young have been found, so scientists are not sure what the adults looked like.

Bagaceratops

(BAG-uh-SAIR-uh-tops)

Bagaceratops was a small dinosaur that grew to about 3 feet (1 meter) in length. This ceratopsian is known from fossils found in Mongolia.

FUN FACT

Several Psittacosauruses probably laid eggs in one nest, like modern ostriches. In this way, they could share the burden of guarding the nest.

Psittacosaurus

(SIT-ah-co-SAWR-us)

Psittacosaurus had a parrot-like beak. Scientists think this primitive ceratopsian was an ancestor of the giant horned dinosaurs that followed.

Protoceratops (PRO-toh-SAIR-uh-tops)

was a primitive ceratopsian that lacked a nose horn. It lived on the dry plains of what is now Asia about 80 million years ago. Protoceratops lived in herds and fed on low-growing shrubs. More than 100 fossil skeletons of this creature have been found in the Gobi Desert in southern Mongolia and northern China.

FACT○SAUR

Scientists have found a fossilized Protoceratops skeleton locked in combat with a meat-eating dinosaur called Velociraptor.

The neck frill was supported by struts of bone and was probably used more to impress a mate than for defense.

Protoceratops had a horny beak somewhat like that of a bird. It lacked a horn on the nose.

The long tail indicates that the four-legged Protoceratops descended from dinosaurs that walked on two legs. They needed this long tail for balance.

25

Chasmosaurus

(KAS-mo-SAWR-us)

Chasmosaurus had a huge neck shield, but much of it consisted of just muscle and skin stretched between bones. This made the shield relatively light and easy to carry.

Einiosaurus

(eye-nee-oh-SAWR-us)

The well-protected Einiosaurus had two straight horns rising from its neck frill and a single, downward-curving horn on its nose.

Centrosaurus

(SEN-tro-SAWR-us)

Centrosaurus was a massive ceratopsian that weighed up to 13 tons (11.8 metric tons). The large nose horn was a powerful weapon. It lived in what is now North America.

FUN FACT

Many ceratopsian fossils are found together. This indicates that they likely moved in large herds, for protection from predators.

Pentaceratops

(PEN-ta-SAIR-uh-tops)

Pentaceratops had an awesome neck frill that could grow up to 10 feet (3 meters) in length. The huge frill was studded with short spikes. Pentaceratops had the largest skull of any land animal that has ever lived.

Pachycephalosaurus

(pack-ee-SEF-ah-low-SAWR-us)

Pachycephalosaurus had an incredibly thick, domed skull surrounded by spikes. It may have used its head as a battering ram to win mates.

Styracosaurus

(sty-RACK-oh-SAWR-us)

Styracosaurus had more spikes and horns on its head than any other ceratopsian. Many of these were long, yet thin. They may have been mainly for display instead of defense.

Leptoceratops

(LEP-to-SAIR-uh-tops)

Leptoceratops was another small, primitive ceratopsian that suvived into the late Cretaceous Period. It could probably stand and even run on its hind legs, which were longer than the front legs.

FUN FACT

Scientists have found Montanoceratops nests. Each nest contained 12 fossilized eggs laid in a spiral pattern.

Montanoceratops

(mon-TAN-oh-SAIR-uh-tops)

Montanoceratops was a primitive ceratopsian that lived in large herds during the late Cretaceous Period. It had a small, simple head frill and claws on its limbs. Fossilized Montanoeceratops bones have been found only in the U.S. state of Montana.

FACT○SAUR

Triceratops bones have been found in vast numbers in Alberta, Canada, where a huge herd was caught in a flood.

Triceratops *(tri-SAIR-uh-tops)* had two horns over its eyes and one horn on its nose. Its name means "three-horned face." A huge, bony frill extended from the back of the skull. Triceratops lived about 65 million years ago in what is now western North America.

The horns over the eyes were sharp, reaching up to 3 feet (1 meter) long. These may have been used in contests for mates, but some horns show damage from such predators as Tyrannosaurus.

The horn on top of the nose was short and thick. A parrotlike beak was used to clip vegetation.

Triceratops had strong, stout legs. It may have charged at threats, like a rhinoceros.

Learn more at www.worldbook.com/dino13

Hadrosaurs

The hadrosaurs (*HAD-ruh-sawrz*) were a highly successful group of plant-eating dinosaurs. They lived during the Cretaceous Period, mainly in what are now Asia and North America. Some, such as the famous Iguanodon (*ih-GWAN-uh-don*), weighed as much as a small elephant.

Hadrosaurs are also known as duck-billed dinosaurs. These creatures had long heads with wide muzzles. Scientists once thought that they lived in swamps and used their muzzles to strain the water for aquatic plants, as many ducks do today. We now know that hadrosaurs lived on dry land and roamed about in large herds.

Unlike many other large plant-eating dinosaurs, hadrosaurs could chew their food. Their jaws were able to move up and down as well as from side to side. They used their wide, toothless beaks for cropping off plant leaves. They had rows of tightly-packed teeth at the back of their mouth that could grind up both soft and coarse plants. These teeth were continually replaced as they wore down or were lost.

Some hadrosaurs had a large crest on their head with passages connected to the nose. Scientists think these dinosaurs could blow air through their crest, making a loud honking noise. They may have used these sounds to attract mates or alert the herd to predators.

Many hadrosaurs had large, mostly hollow crests on the skull (*below*). A hadrosaur could stand on its hind legs and crop plant leaves with its wide, ducklike beak (*opposite*).

31

Abrictosaurus

(uh-BRICK-tuh-SAWR-us)

Abrictosaurus was a plant-eating dinosaur of the early Jurassic Period in what is now southern Africa. It is among the earliest ornithischians to appear in the fossil record.

Camptosaurus

(KAMP-toe-SAWR-us)

Camptosaurus stood on four legs to feed on low-lying plants, but it could also stand on just its hind legs to eat leaves from taller trees. It had leaf-shaped teeth.

Dryosaurus

(DRY-oh-SAWR-us)

Dryosaurus was a slender ornithischian that could run fast on its two hind legs. This may have helped it to escape predators.

FUN FACT

Hadrosaurs had jaws that could move from side to side. This enabled them to chew their leafy food.

FACT ○ SAUR

The name Iguanodon means "iguana tooth." The dinosaur's teeth resembled those of modern iguanas.

Iguanodon *(ig-WAHN-oh-don)* lived about 135 million to 125 million years ago, during the early Cretaceous Period. Discovered in 1825, it was one of the first dinosaur fossils ever found.

Scientists now believe that Iguanodon walked on all fours with its tail stretched out behind it, rather than upright like a kangaroo.

Its sharp, toothless beak was used to nip off leaves and buds, which would be ground up by teeth at the back of the mouth.

Each of Iguanodon's thumbs had a huge spike, which was probably used for defense or to pull tree branches toward the mouth.

Learn more at www.worldbook.com/dino14

Corythosaurus

(co-RITH-oh-SAWR-us)
Corythosaurus had a large, hollow, bony crest on top of its head. The helmet-shaped crest was probably used to make a loud honking noise.

Brachylophosaurus

(BRACK-uh-LOF-o-SAWR-us)
A complete Brachylophosaurus skeleton found in 2000 had been mummified in a sand bank. Its stomach contained fossilized conifers, ferns, and flowers. The skull had a crest of solid bone.

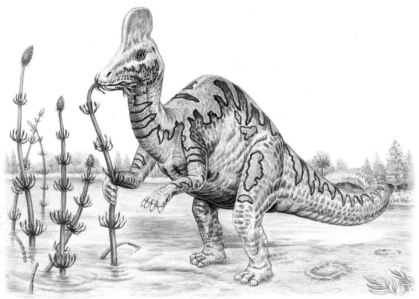

Hadrosaurus

(HAD-roh-SAWR-us)
Hadrosaurus was the first nearly complete fossilized dinosaur skeleton to go on public display. Found in the northeastern United States, it was assembled and displayed in 1868.

Maiasaura *(MY-yah-SAWR-ah)* lived about 80 million to 75 million years ago in what is now Montana. Its name means "good mother lizard," which refers to the large nesting colonies scientists have found. Maiasaura clearly provided care for its young. It lived in large herds that may have migrated with the changing seasons.

The long backbone was stiffened with fibers that helped support its tail, which was used for balance.

Maiasaura could lift itself up on its strong hind legs to reach the tops of trees.

FACT○SAUR

Scientists have found nests with fossilized baby Maiasaura. The adults likely brought food back to the infants, as birds do today.

The wide, toothless beak was ideal for cropping off plants, which were chewed by hundreds of small teeth farther back in the jaw.

Learn more at www.worldbook.com/dino15

Parasaurolophus (PAIR-uh-SOAR-uh-LOAF-us)

was a large duck-billed dinosaur that lived in what is now North America 75 million to 70 million years ago. Like many hadrosaurs, this animal had a large crest on the skull that could make a loud honking noise.

FACT○SAUR

Parasaurolophus varies in the size and shape of its crest, suggesting that different kinds of Parasaurolophus could sound different notes.

Parasaurolophus had broad, three-toed hindfeet to support its huge weight when it reared up to feed on tall plants.

The crest of Parasaurolophus reached 4 feet (1 meter) long. The crest was hollow and connected to the nose, which allowed the animal to make a loud trumpeting sound.

The forefeet were smaller than the hindfeet and had four toes.

Lambeosaurus

(LAM-bee-oh-SAWR-us)
Lambeosaurus was the largest of the duck-billed dinosaurs. It had an elaborate hatchet-shaped head crest. The crest may have been used for display, to attract mates.

Hypacrosaurus

(hi-PACK-roe-SAWR-us)
Hypacrosaurus had up to 40 rows of teeth in its mouth. The teeth wore against each other to stay sharp. A hollow crest may have been used to make loud calls.

Edmontosaurus

(ehd MON toh sawr uhs)
More fossils of Edmontosaurus have been found than those of just about any other dinosaur. Edmontosaurus lacked a head crest. Fossil skin impressions show this dinosaur had clusters of irregularly shaped scales.

Did Dinosaurs Care for Their Young?

For many years, most scientists believed that dinosaurs provided no care for their young. Early *paleontologists* (scientists who study prehistoric life) assumed that dinosaurs laid their eggs and then left the young to fend for themselves, as most modern reptiles do. However, a series of remarkable discoveries have shown that some dinosaurs were caring parents.

The first evidence for dinosaur parenting came in the 1920's. Paleontologists working in Mongolia discovered many fossils of Protoceratops at a single site, including adults, young, and eggs in nests. This discovery showed that Protoceratops parents nested in groups.

Nearby, the scientists found an ostrichlike dinosaur they called Oviraptor, which means "egg robber." Paleontologists gave the dinosaur this name because its skeleton was found atop a nest of eggs, which they thought belonged to Protoceratops. Later, scientists examined the eggs more carefully and discovered that they contained tiny Oviraptors. The Oviraptor was not raiding a Protoceratops nest. Rather, it was sitting among its own eggs, tending them much like a modern bird.

In fact, paleontologists have discovered that birds arose from small, meat-eating dinosaurs much like Oviraptor. Some of the nesting behavior we associate with birds may actually have originated among these dinosaurs.

Still, paleontologists do not believe that all dinosaurs cared for their young. For example, the sauropods were the largest dinosaurs, and each of their eggs was about the size of a bowling ball. However, giant sauropods probably did not care for their young, for the simple reason that a hatchling sauropod could easily have been crushed by the lumbering feet of its own parent! Most hatchling sauropods were likely gobbled up by roving predators, with only a few surviving to become adults.

The most famous dinosaur parent is the hadrosaur Maiasaura, a name which means "good mother lizard." In the 1980's, scientists discovered the dinosaur's fossils

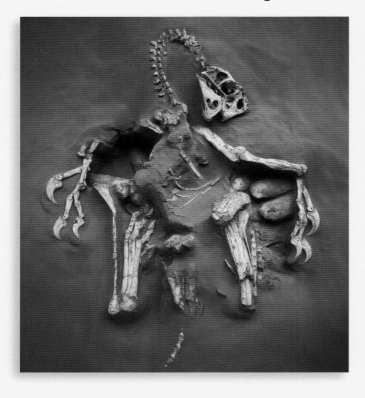

in western Montana, among regularly spaced mounds that were lined with vegetation. These mounds were dinosaur nests. Among the nests, scientists found the remains of eggshells, baby hatchlings, and juveniles. Further study showed that the hatchlings had poorly developed leg muscles, and they probably could not walk. But their teeth showed wear that suggests they were eating the same leafy foods as their parents. Thus, paleontologists think Maiasaura parents must have brought food back to the nest until their hatchlings were old enough to fend for themselves. Many other hadrosaurs may have raised their young in similar fashion.

Paleontologists may never know how many dinosaurs cared for their young, because fossilized nests and eggs are quite rare. Nevertheless, they continue to make remarkable finds that show how dinosaurs lived and reproduced. Scientists may ultimately find that many dinosaurs were caring parents.

Where to Find Dinosaurs

Museums in the United States

ARIZONA

The Arizona Museum of Natural History
http://azmnh.org/Exhibits/dinohall
53 N. Macdonald
Mesa, Arizona 85201

Theropods, sauropods, and other dinosaurs rule at Dinosaur Hall. Visitors can also explore prehistoric Arizona in the Walk Through Time exhibit.

CALIFORNIA

Natural History Museum of Los Angeles County
http://www.nhm.org/site/explore-exhibits
900 Exposition Boulevard.
Los Angeles, California 90007

After you explore the fossils and skeletons in Dinosaur Hall, get a behind-the-scenes look at how the exhibits are made in the Dino Lab.

University of California Museum of Paleontology
http://www.ucmp.berkeley.edu
1101 Valley Life Sciences Building
Berkeley, California 94720

Many of this museum's exhibits are viewable online as well as in person.

COLORADO

The Denver Museum of Nature & Science
http://www.dmns.org
2001 Colorado Boulevard
Denver, Colorado 80205

Dynamic re-creations of ancient environments as well as hands-on fossils tell the story of prehistoric life.

Dinosaur National Monument
http://www.nps.gov/dino
4545 Hwy 40, Dinosaur National Monument
Dinosaur, Colorado 81610

The Dinosaur National Monument is located in both Colorado and Utah. Its world-famous Carnegie Dinosaur Quarry, home to nearly 1,500 dinosaur fossils, is on the Utah side.

CONNECTICUT

Dinosaur State Park
http://www.dinosaurstatepark.org
400 West Street
Rocky Hill, Connecticut 06067

Here you will find one of the largest dinosaur track sites in North America. Visitors can also explore the Arboretum, which contains more than 250 species of plants—many dating back to prehistoric eras.

CONNECTICUT *continued*

The Yale Peabody Museum of Natural History
http://peabody.yale.edu
170 Whitney Avenue
New Haven, Connecticut 06511-8902

Don't miss the Great Hall of Dinosaurs with its famous "Age of Reptiles" mural—one of the largest in the world.

The Natural History Museum of Los Angeles County, Los Angeles, California

GEORGIA

The Fernbank Museum of Natural History
http://www.fernbankmuseum.org
767 Clifton Road NE
Atlanta, Georgia 30307

See a Giganotosaurus and other dinosaurs in the Giants of the Mesozoic exhibit.

ILLINOIS

The Chicago Children's Museum at Navy Pier
http://www.chicagochildrensmuseum.org
700 East Grand Avenue
Chicago, Illinois 60611

Kids of all ages can explore a re-creation of an actual dinosaur dig, where you can search for bones in an excavation pit.

The Discovery Center Museum
http://www.discoverycentermuseum.org
711 North Main Street
Rockford, Illinois 61103

Visitors will enjoy this children's museum's simulated dinosaur dig.

The Field Museum
http://fieldmuseum.org
1400 S Lake Shore Drive
Chicago, Illinois 60605

Chicago's Field Museum is home to Sue, the largest and most complete Tyrannosaurus rex skeleton ever discovered.

INDIANA

The Dinosphere at the Children's Museum of Indianapolis
http://www.childrensmuseum.org/
themuseum/dinosphere
3000 North Meridian Street
Indianapolis, Indiana 46208

Experience the world of the dinosaurs with family digs, fossil preparation, and sensory exhibits.

MAINE

The Maine Discovery Museum
http://www.mainediscoverymuseum.org
74 Main Street
Bangor, Maine 04401

Young visitors to this children's museum can explore the world of paleontology at the museum's new Dino Dig exhibit.

MASSACHUSETTS

The Museum of Science, Boston
http://www.mos.org
1 Science Park
Boston, Massachusetts 02114

A 23-foot- (7-meter-) long Triceratops specimen, found in the Dakota Badlands, is just one of the fascinating fossils on display here.

MICHIGAN

The University of Michigan Museum of Natural History
http://www.lsa.umich.edu/ummnh
1109 Geddes Avenue
Ann Arbor, Michigan 48109

Michigan's largest collection of prehistoric specimens can be found in the Museum of Natural History's rotunda and galleries.

**The Field Museum,
Chicago, Illinois**

The American Museum
of Natural History,
New York City

MINNESOTA

The Science Museum of Minnesota
http://www.smm.org
120 W. Kellogg Boulevard
St. Paul, Minnesota 55102

Do some hands-on fossil exploration at the Paleontology Lab, then get inside the jaws of a giant T. rex to simulate its mighty bite!

NEW MEXICO

The New Mexico Museum of Natural History and Science
http://www.nmnaturalhistory.org
1801 Mountain Road NW
Albuquerque, New Mexico 87104

The Timetracks exhibit covers the Triassic, Jurassic, and Cretaceous periods as part of a journey from the origins of life on Earth to the present day.

NEW YORK

The American Museum of Natural History
http://www.amnh.org
Central Park West at 79th Street
New York, New York 10024

This museum's famous Fossil and Dinosaur halls house nearly 1 million specimens.

NORTH CAROLINA

North Carolina Museum of Natural Sciences
http://naturalsciences.org
11 West Jones Street
Raleigh, North Carolina 27601

Home to Willo the Thescalosaurus, an Acrocanthosaurus, and four fossilized whales.

PENNSYLVANIA

The Academy of Natural Sciences of Drexel University
http://www.ansp.org/visit/exhibits/dinosaur-hall
1900 Benjamin Franklin Parkway
Philadelphia, Pennsylvania 19103

Impressive skeletons of massive dinosaurs stalk Drexel's Dinosaur Hall. Visitors can also visit the fossil lab to learn how fossils are prepared and studied.

The Carnegie Museum of Natural History
http://www.carnegiemnh.org/exhibitions/dinosaurs.html
4400 Forbes Avenue
Pittsburgh, Pennsylvania 15213

The Dinosaurs in the Their Time exhibit features scientifically accurate re-creations of environments from the Age of Dinosaurs, organized chronologically.

SOUTH DAKOTA

The Children's Museum of South Dakota
http://www.prairieplay.org
521 4th Street
Brookings, South Dakota 57006

Meet Mama and Max, a pair of full-sized animatronic T. rex dinosaurs, and try your hand at a dinosaur dig.

TENNESSEE

The Creative Discovery Museum
http://www.cdmfun.org
321 Chestnut Street
Chattanooga, Tennessee 37402
The Creative Discovery Museum's Excavation Station lets young visitors dig their own dinosaur bones.

TEXAS

The Houston Museum of Natural Science
http://www.hmns.org
5555 Hermann Park Drive
Houston, Texas 77030
A world-class Hall of Paleontology includes more than 30 new dinosaurs and many other prehistoric creatures in "action" poses.

UTAH

The Natural History Museum of Utah
http://nhmu.utah.edu
301 Wakara Way
Salt Lake City, Utah 84108
The paleontology collections at Utah's Natural History Museum house more than 30,000 specimens.

VIRGINIA

The Virginia Museum of Natural History
http://www.vmnh.net
21 Starling Avenue
Martinsville, Virginia 24112
Detailed models and interactive features accompany the dinosaur exhibits.

WASHINGTON D.C.

The National Museum of Natural History—Smithsonian Institution
http://www.mnh.si.edu
10th Street & Constitution Avenue NW
Washington, D.C. 20560
Visit the Hall of Paleontology—free of charge—to come face-to-face with dinosaurs, fossil mammals, and fossil plants.

WYOMING

The Wyoming Dinosaur Center
http://www.wyodino.org
110 Carter Ranch Road
Thermopolis, Wyoming 82443
The combined museum and dig site offers daylong digs for visitors of all ages.

The Carnegie Museum of Natural History, Pittsburgh, Pennsylvania

Museums in Canada

ALBERTA

The Royal Tyrrell Museum
http://www.tyrrellmuseum.com
1500 North Dinosaur Trail
Drumheller, Alberta T0J 0Y0, Canada

Tyrannosaurus rex, Triceratops, Quetzalcoatlus (a pterodactyloid), and many other fossils can be found here.

ONTARIO

The Canadian Museum of Nature
http://nature.ca/en/home
240 McLeod Street
Ottawa, Ontario, Canada

Explore the lives—and the eventual extinction—of the dinosaurs in the Fossil Gallery.

The London Children's Museum
http://www.londonchildrensmuseum.ca
21 Wharncliffe Road South
London, Ontario N6J 4G5, Canada

The Dinosaur Gallery includes demonstrations, fossil casts, and replicas of many dinosaurs from the Jurassic Period.

The Royal Ontario Museum
http://www.rom.on.ca
100 Queen's Park
Toronto, Ontario, M5S 2C6, Canada

These exhibits feature dinosaurs and other fossils from the Jurassic and Cretaceous periods.

QUEBEC

The Redpath Museum
http://www.mcgill.ca/redpath
859 Sherbrooke Street West
Montreal, Quebec, Canada

Learn about the animals that roamed prehistoric Quebec as well as about many types of dinosaur.

Museums in the United Kingdom

Dinosaurland Fossil Museum
http://www.dinosaurland.co.uk/
Coombe Street, Lyme Regis
Dorset, DT7 3PY, United Kingdom

Dinosaurland includes a large collection of Jurassic fossils and dinosaur models.

The Dinosaur Museum
http://www.thedinosaurmuseum.com/
Icen Way, Dorchester
Dorset, DT1 1EW, United Kingdom

Highlights include kid-friendly, hands-on computer displays, dinosaur skeletons, and a wide range of fossils.

The National Museum of Scotland
http://www.nms.ac.uk/
Chambers Street
Edinburgh, EH1 1JF, United Kingdom

Allosaurus and Triceratops skeletons are part of a prehistory exhibit, along with dinosaur footprints and a "dino dig" for young visitors.

The Natural History Museum
http://www.nhm.ac.uk/
Cromwell Road, London SW7 5BD

The elaborate dinosaur gallery includes four animatronic dinosaurs.

Oxford University Museum of Natural History
http://www.oum.ox.ac.uk/
Parks Road, Oxford,
OX1 3PW, United Kingdom

The outstanding collection of dinosaur fossils and skeletons includes a Camptosaurus, Cetiosaurus, Eustreptospondylus, Iguanodon, Lexovisaurus, Megalosaurus, and a Metriacanthosaurus.

Museums in Australia

The Australian Museum
http://australianmuseum.net.au
6 College Street Sydney
New South Wales 2010, Australia

A permanent dinosaur exhibit features high-tech interactive displays, animatronic dinosaurs, and a paleontology lab that is open to young visitors.

The Melbourne Museum
http://museumvictoria.com.au/
melbournemuseum
11 Nicholson St. Carlton
Victoria, 3053, Australia

A kid-friendly Dinosaur Walk exhibition brings the prehistoric world to life.

The National Dinosaur Museum
http://www.nationaldinosaurmuseum.com.au
Gold Creek Road and Barton Highway
Nicholls, Australia Capital Terrority 2913

Home to the largest permanent display of dinosaur and other prehistoric fossil material in Australia.

The South Australian Museum
http://www.samuseum.sa.gov.au
North Terrace
Adelaide, South Australia 5000, Australia

Walk through a paleontology collection that includes more than 40,000 specimens.

The Australian Museum, Sydney, Australia *(left)*

The Royal Tyrrell Museum, Drumheller, Canada *(opposite)*

Museums in New Zealand

The Canterbury Museum
http://www.canterburymuseum.com/
Christchurch Central, Christchurch 8013
New Zealand

The Geology gallery features fossils and an introduction to the fearsome marine reptiles of New Zealand's prehistory.

Additional Resources

Books

Dinosaur Discovery: Everything You Need to Be a Paleontologist
by Christopher McGowan and Erica Lyn Schmidt (Simon and Schuster Books for Young Readers, 2011)
Activities and experiments show readers how paleontologists examine ancient fossils.

Dinosaur Mountain: Digging into the Jurassic Age
by Deborah Kogan Ray (Frances Foster Books/Farrar, Straus, Giroux, 2010)
Follow fossil expert Earl Douglass on his 1908 hunt for dinosaur bones, which led to the discovery of several amazing skeletons.

Dinosaurs
by John A. Long (Simon and Schuster Books for Young Readers, 2007)
3-D model imaging helps bring dinosaurs to life in this informative book.

Dinosaurs: The Most Complete, Up-to-Date Encyclopedia for Dinosaur Lovers of All Ages
by Thomas R. Holtz and Luis V. Rey (Random House, 2007)
A reference guide to all things dinosaur, from fossil hunting to evolution.

The Discovery and Mystery of a Dinosaur Named Jane
by Judith Williams (Enslow Publishers, 2008)
This book traces the journey of one dinosaur's skeleton, from discovery to museum.

DVD's

Bizarre Dinosaurs
(National Geographic, 2009)
Paleontologists lead you on a tour of some of the strangest dinosaurs to ever walk the Earth.

Dinosaur Collection
(Discovery-Gaiam, 2011)
Computer-animated simulations paint a vivid picture of dinosaurs and their world.

Dinosaurs Unearthed
(National Geographic, 2007)
Watch the examination of a mummified dinosaur for a new understanding of how dinosaurs looked, moved, and lived.

Index

Photo Credits